SCIENCE ON PATROL

under the
Ground

**Louise and
Richard Spilsbury**

 Gareth Stevens
PUBLISHING

Please visit our website, www.garethstevens.com.
For a free color catalog of all our high-quality books,
call toll free 1-800-542-2595 or fax 1-877-542-2596.

Cataloging-in-Publication Data

Names: Spilsbury, Louise.
Title: Under the ground / Louise and Richard Spilsbury.
Description: New York : Gareth Stevens, 2017. | Series: Science on patrol | Includes index.
Identifiers: ISBN 9781482459845 (pbk.) | ISBN 9781482459869 (library bound) | ISBN 9781482459852 (6 pack)
Subjects: LCSH: Geology--Juvenile literature. | Earth sciences--Juvenile literature.
Classification: LCC QE29.S65 2017 | DDC 550--dc23

First Edition

Published in 2017 by
Gareth Stevens Publishing
111 East 14th Street, Suite 349
New York, NY 10003

Produced for Gareth Stevens by Calcium
Editors: Sarah Eason and Jennifer Sanderson
Designers: Paul Myerscough and Simon Borrough
Picture researcher: Rachel Blount

Picture credits: Cover: Shutterstock: Joe Ravi (t), Salajean (b); Inside: NASA: NASA Goddard/ MODIS Rapid
Response Team 37; Shutterstock: Adwo 17, 26–27, Albund 36, Marco Barone 5, Beboy 15, B Brown 44–45,
Alex Brylov 25, Darkkong 10, Yuttana Jeenamool 31, Michael C. Gray 28, Peter Gudella 39, MarcelClemens 12,
Kenneth Keifer 42–43, Michal Kowalski 16, Natursports 29, Naypong 14, PhotoStock10 13, Michel Piccaya 24,
Rumo 34, Salajean 6–7b, 7t, Bjoern Wylezich 11, Yarygin 35, Igor Zh. 23; USGS: 20; Wikimedia Commons: NASA/
Jefferson Beck 19, Builderpb 21, USGS/W. Chadwick 1, 9, Geophile71 3, 38, Markus Leitner, Bayerisches Rotes
Kreuz, Kreisverband Berchtesgadener Land 8, R.B. Moore, NiBzH 30, North Sullivan Photography, CSIRO 33, U.S.
Geological Survey 4, USGS 18, Alexander Van Driessche 40–41b, Yerpo 41t.

Printed in China
CPSIA compliance information: Batch #CW17GS: For further information contact Gareth Stevens, New York, New York at 1-800-542-2595.

contents

WORKING UNDER THE GROUND

Scientists who study and work beneath the surface of our planet have to cope with a very distinctive and challenging type of habitat. Space under the ground can be extremely limited, and it may also be hot, wet, and dark.

Through Earth

The part of the planet we see is the thin outer skin of rock called the crust. The crust is about 25 miles (40 kilometers) deep. Beneath the crust is a thick layer of hot rocks, called the mantle, which moves very, very slowly. Rock in the crust and mantle can melt into liquid called magma. Magma is the molten rock that erupts from volcanoes. When it cools, the magma hardens into new rock at the surface. The core, forming the center of Earth, is a vast ball of red-hot iron.

Studying under the ground can be very dangerous for scientists, such as these volcano researchers.

Changing Earth

The rock in the outer crust is slowly but constantly changing. Shifts in the crust can make mountains grow. Rock can break into pieces, for example, when water freezes in rock clefts. This is a form of **weathering**. Rivers and wind **erode**, or carry, the pieces of weathered rock from one place to another. This is erosion. Pieces of rock may gradually become buried under others and eventually move so deep that they can become part of new rocks. The process of change from rock to new rock is called the rock cycle.

Seeing Beneath

There is no way that scientists can go under the ground to study most of the planet. The crust is mostly thick, solid rock, although people can get inside through natural gaps or tunnels and holes they make with drills or explosives. Even if scientists could go deeper, they would soon feel the effects of searingly hot temperatures and high **pressure**, which is the push of the millions of tons of rock surrounding them.

Under the ground is a hidden world that scientists want to know more about.

CAVE EXPLORATION

Caves or caverns are hollow places underground that are big enough for people to go inside and explore. They range from single chambers measuring tens of feet across to vast systems of caves interlinked with shafts and tunnels, measuring hundreds of miles.

Cave Formation

Nearly all caves are created naturally by weathering. They usually form in rock called limestone. Limestone mixes easily in rainwater containing **dissolved** carbon dioxide gas. This makes a mild **acid** that dissolves **minerals** in the rock. When water trickles underground through cracks, it can wear away so much rock over long periods that it forms vertical potholes, horizontal tunnels, and caves. The weathered minerals can also stick together in caves, forming new structures called stalactites and stalagmites. Caves sometimes form naturally without weathering, too, for example, when hot magma melts holes through solid rock as it passes through.

Caves take thousands of years to form through natural processes.

Dangerous Caves

Caves can be dangerous places to explore. Scientists need to be skilled in using climbing ropes and must be able to lower themselves into a cave and to pull themselves out of it. Inside caves, people can trip and fall on the uneven floors and hit their heads and limbs. Cave roofs and tunnel walls can crumble and collapse in on themselves. That is why wearing a protective helmet is essential. It is also important to have a reliable headlight so scientists can see where they are going. Despite this, it is easy to become lost in caves and cave systems. There may be few landmarks to help with navigation, maps may be inaccurate, and changes in level and direction can be confusing in the darkness.

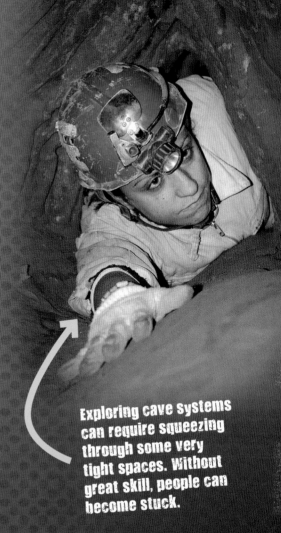

Exploring cave systems can require squeezing through some very tight spaces. Without great skill, people can become stuck.

Not Alone

Scientists may come face to face with a range of interesting animals as they explore caves. These include:
• Bats that roost hanging upside down from cave ceilings.
• White, blind fish living in cave rivers.
• Glowworms that dangle from the ceiling. Their light attracts flies they catch and eat.
• Giant, poisonous centipedes that can kill bats and give people a nasty bite.

UNDERGROUND HAZARDS

Under the ground, scientists and their teams are on their own, with no support. They need to be prepared for many dangers, from volcanic eruptions to flooding. They know that it might be tricky for others to rescue them if they have problems far beneath the surface.

Poisonous Gases

Under the ground there are many poisonous gases. That is why scientists often need to wear sealed breathing masks and come equipped with tanks of oxygen to breathe. Harmful underground gases include hydrogen sulfide, which stinks of rotten eggs and irritates the eyes and throat. In caves, the oxygen levels in the air can be too low to breathe, because air does not move in and out and refresh underground. When people have too little oxygen and too much carbon dioxide or carbon monoxide, they can get headaches and pass out.

It can be trickier to rescue people who get injured or get sick under the ground than at the surface because they can be helped out only through tight spaces.

Waterlogged

One of the problems with working underground is that water from the surface collects there. Some caves and tunnels are permanently flooded. During heavy storms, even normally dry caves can flood rapidly. Underground streams can swell into raging rivers that can drown people. The wetness and cold under the ground can chill people and cause hypothermia, too. This is when people lose heat too fast, their brains become confused, and eventually, their hearts may stop working. Scientists need to be prepared to avoid hypothermia by wearing warm and waterproof clothes, hats, and gloves in cold, damp places under the ground.

SCIENCE PATROL SURVIVAL

It is important for scientists working in caves to drink water regularly to avoid becoming **dehydrated**. Water is vital for body processes, from digesting food to urination and sweating.

How does sweating work to keep people cool? Why would being in a warm, damp cave be a problem? Explain your answers.

Scientists check the levels of poisonous gases from inside a volcano. The yellow sulfur is a sign of the presence of poisonous sulfurous gases.

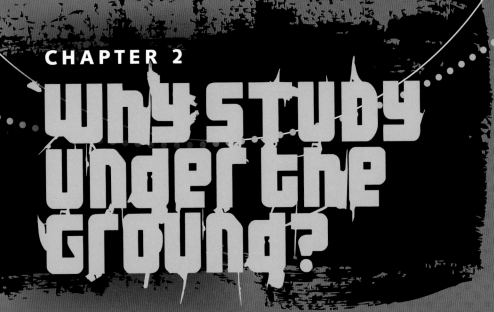

CHAPTER 2

why study under the ground?

Many different types of scientists study the world beneath our feet to learn more about a variety of things, including fossils and **fossil fuels**, mineral **resources**, such as gemstones, and how volcanoes and earthquakes happen.

Fossils

Fossils are the remains of plants and animals that lived on Earth millions of years ago. Fossil remains are usually preserved in layers of rock underground, although weathering and erosion may bring them to the surface. Fossils are important because we have no written records of life on Earth from the distant past. This is because people were not around to write them or did not yet write.

Scientists unearth fossils under the ground and piece them together to construct dinosaurs and other animals, so we can learn more about these ancient creatures.

Most fossils discovered are of shelled animals, such as this ammonite.

By studying fossils, scientists can figure out what plants and animals lived on Earth in the past and how they lived. They can also discover how animals **evolved**: how species develop and gradually change from one form to another. For example, **paleontologists** studying early birds saw that they had traces of feathers, but they also had a tail, claws, and fingers like reptiles. This tells them that modern birds likely evolved from reptiles.

How Fossils Formed

By studying fossils, scientists have figured out how fossils form and, therefore, where they are likely to find more fossils. Most fossils form in sedimentary rock. For example, ammonites were sea animals that had a spiral shell. They lived from around 400 million years ago. When an ammonite died, its body sank to the ocean floor, where its soft parts rotted away or were eaten by other animals. The hard shell was gradually buried in layers of **sediment**. Over hundreds of thousands of years, minerals from the water seeped into the shell, where they replaced the minerals in the shell. Under pressure from the weight of the rock above, the minerals turned to hard rock in exactly the shape of the ammonite shell, and a fossil was formed.

MINERAL RESOURCES

Many vital resources that people need, such as minerals and fuels, are found under the ground. Researchers have an important role to play in finding and studying these resources and their uses.

Minerals

Minerals are solid, **inorganic** substances that form and are found in rocks. There is a huge variety of minerals, from those that form **crystal** shapes and are often made into expensive jewelry, such as diamonds, to more common minerals such as quartz, which is found in sand and used to make glass. Scientists find different minerals and use tests to identify what they are. For example, some scientists search for grains of gold in **samples** of soil. Some scientists scratch minerals with different materials to test their hardness. This helps them identify the minerals. The hardest mineral is diamond.

Scientists know where to look for the rare places where there are large enough deposits of gold to be mined profitably.

By studying the properties of minerals, scientists can figure out what they could be used for. For example, they discovered that aluminum is light, easy to shape, and does not rust like iron does. This makes it ideal for constructing airplane and vehicle bodies, and soda cans. The metal copper was discovered to **conduct** electricity well, so it is now used inside electrical wires.

Fossil Fuels

Fossil fuels are fuels such as oil, natural gas, and coal that form from the remains of animals and plants that lived millions of years ago. Buried underground and under intense heat and pressure from deep within Earth, these remains have become sources of power. These fossil fuels are used as energy sources for vehicles, including cars and airplanes, power stations, and other machines. Scientists help locate sources of fossil fuel under the ground, figure out how big they are, and design the machines to bring the fuels to the surface.

Scientists help find oil and also study how its use is contributing to climate change.

VOLCANOES and EARTHQUAKES

Volcanoes and earthquakes are natural events that can cause deadly disasters. Scientists study them to find out how, where, and why they happen, and to figure out if they can predict when such violent events occur. By predicting them, they can warn people to move to a place of safety before disaster strikes.

Earthquakes

Earthquakes can create large and dangerous cracks in the surface of Earth.

An earthquake happens when an area of land shakes and shudders violently. Large earthquakes can topple buildings, crack roads, and break bridges. Earthquakes occur because Earth's crust is split into large pieces, called tectonic plates, which fit together like a jigsaw puzzle. The plates float like giant rafts on the hot, bubbling rock of the mantle beneath them. They are moving slowly all the time, sliding past one another and bumping into each other. An earthquake can happen when two plates push against each other and then suddenly slip apart. Scientists study the **plate boundaries** where tectonic plates meet in order to find out where earthquakes are more likely to happen.

If scientists can spot signs that a volcano might erupt, they can warn people to leave the area.

Volcanoes

When a volcano erupts, it spurts out poisonous gas, hot ash, and hot magma, which is called lava when it leaves the ground. These flow down the sides of the volcano onto land below. Large volcanic eruptions can cause terrible destruction, burning everything and everyone in their path. Scientists have learned that volcanoes happen where tectonic plates meet, and above places where the magma is extremely hot. Magma squeezes up toward the surface, melting rock that gets in its way, making a tunnel through the crust. Near the hard surface of the crust, it becomes stuck and more magma builds up beneath it. When the pressure from below becomes too great, the magma bursts through the crust. The volcano erupts. **Geologists** study volcanoes to try to predict future eruptions, and to gather information about the structure of Earth.

Soils and Water

To most people, soil just looks like dirt. To scientists, there is a huge variety of soils, formed from different minerals and in various ways. Soil is necessary for growing the crops that feed the world. Beneath the ground, there is also **groundwater**. This is a vital source of water for plants and for supplying one-third of the world's population with drinking water.

Soil Samples

Soil is a precious resource because it is used to grow plants for food. Plants release oxygen during the process of **photosynthesis**, by which they make food. People need oxygen to breathe. Soil is made up of tiny grains of weathered rocks and particles of natural waste, such as rotted leaves. Water and air collect in the spaces between these particles. Scientists identify different types of soil by testing samples of them for things such as color, texture, and the minerals they contain.

Scientists study samples of soil in a laboratory.

As well as studying the land, soil scientists also research its water resources.

Grading Groundwater

Groundwater forms when rain and water from melted snow seep under the ground and collect in gaps in the rock. This water collects in underground streams or pools in **porous** rocks. Rock that contains groundwater that can be pumped or lifted to the surface is called an **aquifer**. Sometimes, water comes to the surface naturally in springs. Scientists study groundwater sources to see how quickly they are being used up and how they are being polluted, for example by industrial waste. They also investigate ways to clean **contaminated** water and make it safe to use again.

SCIENCE PATROL SURVIVAL

By studying soils, scientists can help people. For example, they test soils to see how acidic they are. Only a few plants grow well in acidic soils. Scientists develop substances that can be added to soils to make them less acidic.

How could this help farmers and gardeners? How could this increase the crops in an area and help feed more people?

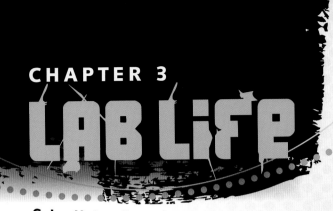

CHAPTER 3

LAB LIFE

Scientists often go on field trips to different places of interest to study under the ground. However, they also do much of their research in laboratories in fixed places.

Range of Laboratories

Some laboratories are small buildings, occupied only when geologists are in residence. Others are large enough to have many rooms and permanent staff members managing facilities. They may have places for scientific study, as well as classrooms for teaching visiting students, conference halls where scientists present their findings to other scientists, and libraries full of books, journals, and **geological** maps. The biggest labs may have dormitories and canteens for scientists and support staff, such as technicians, to live while they work.

Being located near a volcano allows scientists to see remarkable volcanic structures, such as this horn-shaped hornito, which formed when lava flowed upward and cooled.

Lab Locations

Some laboratories are found in larger institutions, such as universities and colleges in towns and cities, but many are located near features of geological interest. For example, there are laboratories at sedimentary rock formations where many interesting fossils can be found near the surface. There are also labs near oil and natural gas deposits. Some of the most remarkable geological events—earthquakes and volcanoes—happen at particular places around the globe. Volcanic observatories are laboratories located within sight of volcanoes. Scientists based there can spot the signs of possible eruptions and study their impacts. These labs need to be located where scientists and others can evacuate the area safely and quickly along roads or tracks.

Airborne Lab

Sometimes, scientists need to go up in the air to study rocks over very large areas. In these cases, they can use airborne laboratories that not only have specialist machinery but also computers and monitors. The computers calculate and display what the machines are detecting and communicate information to and from laboratories on the ground.

These scientists are using machines in an airborne laboratory to detect water-filled holes hidden beneath the thick Arctic ice.

LAB TOUR

No two geological laboratories are exactly alike. Some are specialized spaces with equipment that does particular jobs, such as electron microscopes to look closely at the structure of minerals. Others are more general and contain a range of instruments useful to many scientists studying on and under the ground. Here are a few of the things you might find in a geological lab:

Weighing machines: For many scientific tests, exact measurements of samples can be critical, so labs have a range of balances to weigh rocks and soils. Rock samples are often heavy, so labs have strong benches and storage racks, shelves, and cupboards for samples, too.

Preparation areas: Rocks brought into labs from the field may first be prepared before analysis. Rocks are sometimes washed in sinks and sawed into very thin sections to let light through. This enables minerals to be viewed more easily. Soils may be dried in ovens to remove moisture before weighing and studying soil components, from minerals to **bacteria**.

This scientist is collecting a device used to test water for pollution that has been at a sampling site for a month. He will take it to the lab for analysis.

Lenses and microscopes: Geological labs have simple hand lenses and binocular microscopes for scientists to look at the surface of samples. More powerful microscopes may have different light sources to help study rocks, because some minerals glow in particular colors under **ultraviolet** light.

Specialized machines: Scientists can carry out basic tests for the hardness of rocks by scratching them or seeing if they react with acid. They use expensive machines to apply pressure to materials, too. This can help test whether soils will sink if structures such as towers or airports are built on them.

Computers: Labs have powerful computers to analyze **data**. They may have the ability to upload data from machines in the field, such as **sensors** measuring ground movements for signs of forthcoming earthquakes.

This scientist is using a triaxial compression machine that pushes very hard on sand, soil, or soft rock samples. It measures how much force it takes to make the samples change shape.

Underground Lab

Some laboratories are built in unused mines. The mines are dug out to become a range of chambers that are fitted with high-tech instruments and machines. These labs are far more pleasant than the mines were for miners in the past, with air conditioning, strong lighting, and comfortable work spaces.

Advantages of Depth

The Sanford Underground Research Facility (SURF) in South Dakota has several levels. The deepest is as deep as 6.5 Eiffel Towers. Scientists work there partly because there is low **radiation**. Earth's surface is constantly bombarded with radiation from the sun, cell phone towers, and other sources. The radiation can make it impossible to use extremely sensitive machines, so the thick, hard rock around the laboratory blocks the unwanted radiation. Deep under the ground, there are also naturally higher temperatures and greater pressure than at the surface, so scientists can test rocks and how living things, such as bacteria, survive these conditions.

Beyond Our Planet

Some scientists go under the ground to study the **universe**. Everything is made of **matter**, which is made of **atoms**. Scientists believe that there must be invisible dark matter far smaller than atoms in space. They hope their incredibly sensitive machines may be able to detect moving particles of dark matter. Once they have proved dark matter exists, then they can start to understand how stars made the chemicals that we and other living things are made from.

Some scientists study under the ground to learn more about the universe far above us.

SCIENCE PATROL SURVIVAL

The Sanford Lab's Emergency Response Team is always on call and practices underground rescue techniques each week. The team has special evacuation techniques, such as releasing a harmless but smelly chemical into the air that blows through all the caves and tunnels to warn workers of danger.

Why do you think smell is a useful warning underground? Why might people need to evacuate from an underground laboratory? Is it fair to ask people to risk their lives in helping scientists who choose to work underground? Explain your answers.

CHAPTER 4

OUT and ABOUT

Scientists who study under the ground do not usually do so in places where many people live because there are buildings, car lots, and other structures covering the surface. They usually go on patrol in remote places where there are large areas of undisturbed land. That means they need vehicles and equipment to help them move around.

Getting There

Driving on rough **terrain** demands a vehicle that can cope with rocky trails covered with bumps and holes. Most scientists use an SUV or a four-wheel-drive (4x4) vehicle. These have higher wheels than ordinary cars, so they can hold the body of the vehicle away from rocks that might damage the underside. Scientists always check a vehicle carefully before setting out to somewhere remote. They carry a full tool kit and spare tires so they can fix any breakdowns or damage, because they will be too far from a garage to get a mechanic to help them.

The wheels on a 4x4 are wide to spread the heavy load of the vehicle and the equipment inside, and to better grip surfaces, such as wet soil or loose sand.

Navigation

Scientists on patrol in remote regions carry a compass, a map, and a **Global Positioning System (GPS)** device. A compass needle always points north, and a map has things such as high hills marked on it to help with navigation. With a map and a compass, people can figure out directions. GPS units use **satellite** links to find locations.

Scientists use radios and satellite phones to contact people in case of an emergency and to send data back to the lab.

SCIENCE PATROL SURVIVAL

When scientists set off to remote places to study under the ground, they may be gone for several days. As well as equipment they need for research, they have to carry tents, sleeping bags, food, and medical supplies. In addition to carrying out their work, they have to find somewhere safe to stay and cope with bad weather and often extreme heat or cold. They also have to be ready to cope with having an accident far from the hospital.

How do you think dealing with these daily challenges might affect scientists as they work? Give reasons for your answers.

GEOLOGISTS' KIT

When geologists set out to study an area of ground, they take a variety of equipment with them. These tools allow a geologist to **excavate**, analyze, and store samples from under the ground so they can study rocks, minerals, and other important geological formations.

Basic Checklist

Almost all field geologists will have most of the following equipment:

Geological hammer: This will be made of steel so that it will not splinter like regular household hammers. Geological hammers have a flat face and often a chisel end for splitting rocks. The hammer can be used to hit wide, thin chisels, too, that carefully split sedimentary rocks into layers.

Notebooks and computers: Geologists may record finds with anything from descriptions in notebooks and diagrams in a sketchbook to digital photos and videos. Sample collection locations are recorded on maps or by using GPS via smartphones or computers.

Bags and boxes: Scientists usually stow labeled samples in plastic bags and boxes.

Safety gear: Scientists need to wear goggles to protect their eyes from chips or shards of rock that can fly off when rock is hammered or chiseled. They wear protective gloves, hard-top boots, helmets, and knee pads to prevent injuries to their bodies from hard rocks.

These geologists are collecting rock samples in a remote region of Pilbara, Australia.

Complex Kit

Other equipment used by geologists is more complex and depends on the job at hand. It may include portable ground-radar machines that transmit radio waves underground and detect how they are **reflected**. The machines can locate different types of rock and rock formations below the surface. Samples of rock can be taken from underground using special drilling machines. These are powerful devices usually mounted on vehicles with caterpillar tracks. The machines push steel tubes into rock and trap cores of rock inside when the tubes are pulled to the surface.

ON A FOSSIL DIG

Before starting a fossil dig, scientists need to locate some fossils. Sometimes, they search in an area near where fossils have been found before. At other times, weathering that wears away the soil uncovers a fossil. In some cases, a construction company digging deep into the ground discovers fossils.

Excavation Tools

The first job is to remove enough rock to see how big the fossil is, while being careful to leave enough rock around the fossil to protect it. Scientists may use bulldozers and spades to dig away large chunks of rock and soil. They then use a rock pick to take rock and dirt layers off the top of the fossils. They use a rock hammer and chisel to break off pieces of rock around the fossil. Lastly, they use a brush to remove the layers of dust coating the fossil. They dig up the fossil and the rock around it in one large section, taking care not to damage the fossil as they dig.

Wrapped Up

Scientists wrap fossils in bandages covered with plaster to protect them while they are transported to the lab. There are often many fossil parts in an area, so each has to be labeled and placed carefully in a box that has soft padding for protection. In the lab, scientists remove the plaster and gently chip, scrape, and brush away remaining dirt and rock from the specimen. They cover it with a special glue to make the fossil bones strong. Finally, they assemble the parts together to make as complete a model as possible.

Paleontologists measure or draw and take pictures of the fossils they discover. This helps them later piece together animals in the lab.

It is a long, slow job to remove fossils from under the ground.

SCIENCE PATROL SURVIVAL

In 2016, paleontologists discovered fossils of a crocodile-sized animal that lived 242 million years ago in China. Its hammer-shaped skull helped it feed on underwater plants, making it the first known vegetarian reptile to live in the sea. Scientists made a copy of its jaw from modeling clay and toothpicks to learn how it fed and to see how teeth in the upper and lower jaw locked together.

Do you think it is important to study fossils? What do you think new discoveries like this plant-eating reptile might teach scientists about life on Earth in the past?

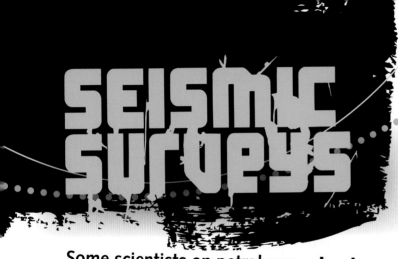

SEISMIC SURVEYS

Some scientists on patrol use **seismic** surveys to explore beneath the ground to find supplies of oil and natural gas and to get a picture of geological formations underground.

Seismic Waves

Scientists must first locate an area of land containing the types of rock that are usually found near natural gas and oil deposits. Then they begin a seismic survey. In a seismic survey, they first generate shock waves, or seismic waves, on the surface. Small, explosive charges of dynamite set off in holes drilled into the ground between 10 and 150 feet (3 and 45 meters) deep cause these waves.

A vibroseis truck has a large metal plate on its underside that is lowered onto the ground so it supports the entire weight of the truck. The plate then vibrates to create seismic waves that travel into the ground.

Large vehicles, called Vibroseis trucks, can also trigger seismic waves. They are fitted with metal plates that are lowered onto the ground where they vibrate strongly. A single vibrator truck can generate large amounts of force, but more often, four or five trucks are used together to create more shock waves.

At the Surface

The seismic waves travel deep into the ground. When they meet something like a pool of oil or a different layer of rock below the surface, the waves are reflected to the surface in different ways. At the surface, a network of seismic sensors are spread over the ground to measure the waves. In some cases, there can be as many as 100,000 sensors over a single field. Scientists use data compiled by the sensors to analyze the time it takes for the seismic waves to reflect off formations below the surface and return to the ground. Using this information they can create a **3-dimensional** map of the layers underground. This helps them figure out where there are oil or natural gas sources large enough to be worth the cost of building oil rigs to extract the fuels.

Scientists use a computer to study data collected by sensors in a seismic survey.

CHAPTER 5

CUTTING-EDGE TECHNOLOGY

Scientists have many types of high-tech equipment to help them study under the ground. Some equipment is used to complete research into rocks, minerals, and the processes in which they form and change over time.

Rock Dating

Figuring out the relative ages of sedimentary rocks is easy for geologists because the younger rocks form on top of the older ones. However, it is trickier to know the exact age of rocks. Scientists use radiodating machines to figure out ages. These machines measure amounts of particular **radioactive** elements in rocks. Over time, these elements decay, or break down, into other elements at a regular speed, rather like a ticking clock. Scientists compare the amount of the original element left in the rock with the speed at which it decays to figure out the age.

Crystal Formation

It is impossible for scientists to get deep enough in Earth's mantle to witness the birth of a diamond or other crystals because of the high temperature and pressure. However, scientists can study processes that happen deep under the ground using machines that artificially make crystals. Devices called HTPT machines are some of the most powerful anvils, or presses, on Earth. They compress graphite, the substance that makes up the lead in pencils, into diamonds. Other machines have a small diamond in a low pressure chamber filled with natural gas. When microwaves are fired at the gas and it is heated to 3,632 degrees Fahrenheit (2,000 degrees Celsius), carbon atoms stick to the diamond and make a perfect sheet of new diamond on top.

Hydraulic fracturing allows people to get at hard-to-reach oil and natural gas deposits and is used in nine out of ten natural gas wells in the United States. However, some countries debate its use because fracking transports huge amounts of water to the fracking site, at significant environmental cost.

Hydraulic Fracturing

Another technology, called hydraulic fracturing, or "fracking," is a technique scientists developed to extract natural gas and oil from shale rock. Shale rock is a fine-grained, muddy, sedimentary rock. With hydraulic fracturing, people drill down under the ground, either vertically or horizontally. Then they shoot millions of gallons of a mixture of water, sand, and chemicals through a pipe directly at the rock under high pressure. This creates small breaks called fissures—fracturing, or splitting apart, the rock. The fissures allow the oil and gas to flow out of the shale and out to the head of the well. The term "fracking" refers to how the rock is fractured apart by the high-pressure mixture.

Volcano and Earthquake Sensing

Scientists use a variety of technology to learn more about volcanoes and earthquakes. This enables scientists to understand them better and also to figure out ways to predict them sooner in order to keep people safe.

Seismographs

A seismograph is a machine that makes a record of the seismic waves caused by an earthquake. Seismographs are equipped with electromagnetic sensors that convert movements under the ground into electrical signals. The seismograph processes and records the electrical signals and produces a record on a display screen or paper printout. The record is called a seismogram. Scientists can study seismograms to monitor earthquakes and volcanoes. For example, long or **low-frequency** earthquakes are caused by cracks resonating as magma and gases move toward the surface. They can be a sign that a volcanic eruption is going to happen.

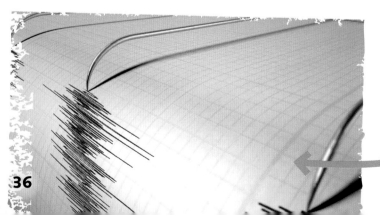

The seismic waves caused by an earthquake are recorded as red lines on a seismograph.

Satellites can record images from space, like this one of ash plumes from a volcano.

Satellite Imagery

Scientists also use satellite imagery to monitor volcanoes. This is called remote sensing. They can use satellite images to check how much heat a volcano is giving off. Increased heat means an upwelling of magma and a possible increase in the risk of an eruption. Scientists can look to see if the ground is deforming by checking images of an area taken at different times. A satellite can also detect if the ground is being uplifted, or rising, by measuring the distance between the satellite and the ground.

Spectrometers

If the quantity of sulfur dioxide in gases seeping from a **dormant** volcano increases, this can signal the start of an eruption. Scientists can study gases released near volcanoes by collecting samples and taking them back to the lab for analysis. In order to study gases without having to go near a potentially dangerous volcano, some **volcanologists** use a special type of spectrometer. A correlation spectrometer is designed to measure the amount of sulfur dioxide in the air or in a volcanic ash cloud or plume. It works by comparing the amount of solar ultraviolet light absorbed by sulfur dioxide in the air to a base standard.

Robots

Robots are machines that move and can be programmed to perform tasks and gather information from their surroundings. A great advantage of robots is that they can go to places that could be very dangerous or impossible for humans to go to. Scientists working under the ground or studying volcanoes use several different types of robot to help them do their research.

Robots are used to take images of volcanoes, such as this close-up of lava inside the Marum volcano crater on Vanuatu Island in the Pacific Ocean.

If a robot is damaged in a dangerous underground mine, it can be replaced.

Volcanic Images

Scientists cannot venture close enough to an erupting volcano to get a good view inside. The intense heat and poisonous gases are highly dangerous. Instead, scientists send drones to take images for them. Drones are flying robots that can be controlled either **autonomously** by onboard computers or by a person using a remote control on the ground or in another vehicle. Scientists have been able to take video footage inside active and highly dangerous volcanoes using drones fitted with high-definition cameras. The drones can be flown close to the toxic gases and boiling lava. Although they eventually burn up, they are able to send back video footage and photos that help scientists learn more about volcanoes.

Using Robots

Some science labs are set up in old underground mines, which can be dangerous to explore. Scientists use robots to investigate these abandoned mines. Groundhog is a wheeled robot that is equipped with **lasers** that can judge distance. It uses the lasers to view the network of tunnels in a mine in order to create detailed maps. MOLE is a tube-shaped robot that crawls through narrow tunnels. It is attached by a cable to the surface through which it sends back digital data to tell scientists at the surface more about the mine. MOLE has sensors that can detect chemicals that may indicate the presence of potentially explosive gases underground. It also has a video camera that can collect images of its surroundings.

CHAPTER 6

AMAZING DISCOVERIES

As well as learning more about fossils, the way volcanoes and earthquakes occur, and minerals underground, scientists have made some remarkable discoveries, including giant crystals, strange animals, and supervolcanoes.

Crystal Caves

Crystals are minerals that have the space to grow into distinctive shapes. This is because the minerals they consist of harden and dry out from chemicals that are dissolved in liquid or present in hot magma.

Crystals in the Cave of Crystals, Naica, Mexico, are some of the largest crystals ever found.

Scientists have figured out that giant crystals found in the Cave of Crystals, a cave 1,000 feet (305 meters) underground beneath a mine in Mexico, formed from gypsum. Gypsum is a mineral that is used to make plaster for walls. Some of the crystals in this cave are more than 39 feet (12 meters) long, 13 feet (4 meters) in diameter, and 55 tons (50 tonnes) in weight. They are 500,000 years old. There is a magma chamber under the cave that helped the crystals form. It makes the Cave of Crystals so hot that the scientists who first explored it in 2006 had to wear refrigerated suits.

Many of the animals that scientists have found in deep caves, like this cave beetle, are blind because there is no need for sight in the darkness.

Strange Animals

Beneath an area of land in southeast Romania, close to the Black Sea, is a cave that no one had ever entered before 1986. After it was discovered by miners looking for a site for a power plant, a Romanian scientist was the first to explore it. It is dangerous to reach, pitch black, and the air there is full of poisonous gases. Despite such obstacles, Movile Cave is also crawling with life. There are unique animals such as leeches, snails, spiders, water scorpions, woodlice, and centipedes, which have never been seen before. No water or nutrients reach the cave from above, but scientists discovered that food chains here start with a floating mat of bacteria, which gets its energy from chemical reactions. Movile is the only cave whose ecosystem is known to be supported in this way.

Supervolcanoes

A supervolcano is a volcano with deposits measuring greater than 240 cubic miles (1,000 cubic kilometers) in an eruption. This is thousands of times larger than normal volcanic eruptions. Supervolcanoes differ from normal eruptions in several ways, but mainly because no human has ever seen one happen.

Finding Supervolcanoes

Scientists have identified where supervolcanoes have erupted by the evidence they leave behind. For example, a supervolcano eruption forms a large depression, or dip, in the ground called a caldera, rather than the cone shape most volcanoes form. A supervolcano often has a ridge of higher land around it, and supervolcanoes do not erupt very often. Eruptions are usually hundreds of thousands of years apart. One of the ways scientists figure out where supervolcanoes are today is by locating huge magma chambers under the ground.

Yellowstone

Yellowstone in Wyoming is a supervolcano. There have been three huge eruptions there in the last 3 million years. The last one was 630,000 years ago. It released such a huge amount of material that it made the ground collapse, creating the 34 mile by 50 mile (55 kilometer by 80 kilometer) caldera that can be seen there today. Yellowstone lies above a volcanic hot spot, an area of Earth's crust where magma is rising and an unusually high amount of heat flows.

There are hot springs and geysers in Yellowstone National Park, where groundwater heated by the chambers of magma under the ground comes out at the surface.

Keeping It Checked

Scientists already knew about one chamber of magma below Yellowstone, but in 2015, they discovered a second, much larger reservoir of magma. There is enough magma in it to fill the Grand Canyon more than 11 times over. This sounds alarming, but a super-eruption at Yellowstone or anywhere else is unlikely in the near future. Even so, scientists are monitoring the magma activity underneath Yellowstone National Park. They check volcanic activity, such as ground deformation, stream flow, and temperatures, and they make models of how far the ash from a super-eruption could spread.

Patrolling the Future

In the future, it could be even more important for science patrols to carry out research under the ground. One of the major issues they will be looking at is the pollution and protection of groundwater sources.

Groundwater Supplies

Earth's supply of freshwater is limited and there are already serious water shortages in many countries across the world.

The demand for water is increasing as the population grows and, to make matters worse, the amount of water available to people is being further reduced by pollution. Scientists study aquifers, how quickly they are being used up, and what causes them to be polluted. In the future, they will look to improve the technologies with which they gather data. It is likely that scientists will use more and more robots to collect data and samples underground and relay the information back to them above the surface.

Aquifers deep under the ground help irrigate vast fields of crops in countries like the United States. Scientists are helping safeguard these vital water supplies for the future.

Future Science

Scientists around the world share information about their discoveries under the ground. By doing so they figure out how accurate their findings are and the best ways to advise governments and countries about how, for example, to reduce the use of water we take from aquifers and how to protect them from pollution. For example, scientists calculate it will take 6,000 years for the Ogallala Aquifer in the high plains of the United States to refill if it is used up. This region supplies at least one-fifth of the annual U.S. harvest, so scientists are helping people manage demands on the aquifer.

SCIENCE PATROL SURVIVAL

Working under the ground is challenging, difficult, and sometimes even dangerous. Scientists need somewhere to work productively and live and relax comfortably. Imagine you are going to design your own underground lab. What will you include in it?

- *How big will it be? What rooms and facilities will it have?*
- *How many labs will you include and what will they be used to study?*
- *How will it be built or delivered deep underground?*
- *How will it cope with the extreme pressure and sometimes heat below the surface?*
- *What recreation facilities will you include?*

Glossary

3-dimensional describes an object that has height, width, and depth, like any object in the real world

acid a substance that is very strong and can damage surfaces

aquifer an underground layer of porous rock, sediment, or soil that holds water

atoms the smallest units of an element

autonomously working by itself

bacteria tiny living things that can cause disease

boreholes deep, narrow holes made in the ground, especially to locate water or oil

climate change changes in the world's weather patterns caused by human activity

conduct to transmit or pass on

contaminated made dirty or poisonous

crystal a hard, solid form of a mineral

data facts and statistics

dehydrated describes something that has had its water content removed

dissolved mixed with a liquid to become part of the liquid

dormant describes something that has not been active for a long period

erode to wear away

evolved developed and changed gradually over long periods of time

excavate to dig up

fossil fuels fuels such as oil or natural gas, formed from plants and animals that died millions of years ago

geological to do with the study of rocks and soil

geologists scientists who study rocks and soil

geysers natural hot springs that spray steam and boiling water into the air

Global Positioning System (GPS) a system that uses signals from satellites in space to locate positions on Earth

groundwater water held underground in the soil or in pores and crevices in rock

inorganic describes something that is not and never was alive

lasers very narrow beams of highly concentrated light

low-frequency describes an earthquake with slow, rumbling movements rather than fierce shocks

matter something that occupies space, has mass, and can exist as a solid, liquid, or gas

minerals substances in nature that do not come from living things

paleontologists scientists who study fossils

photosynthesis the process by which plants make food from carbon dioxide and water using energy from sunlight

plate boundaries where tectonic plates meet

porous full of small holes

pressure a pushing force

radiation energy in the form of waves or particles

radioactive describes something that has a powerful and dangerous form of energy called radiation

reflected bounced back

resources things that people need or use, such as oil and fresh water

samples representative items or parts from a larger whole or group

satellite an electronic device high in space that moves around Earth

sediment material such as stones and sand

seismic relating to movements of the Earth's crust

sensors devices that detect and measure things, such as the amount of a particular gas in the air

terrain land or area of ground

ultraviolet invisible beams of light within sunlight that can damage skin

universe everything that exists, including the whole of space and everything within it

volcanologists scientists who study volcanoes

weathering the breaking up of rock by the rain, wind, or extremes of temperature

For more information

Books

Brooks, Susie. *Earthquakes and Volcanoes* (Where on Earth?). New York, NY: PowerKids Press, 2015.

Leavitt, Amie Jane. *The Science Behind Wonders of the Earth: Cave Crystals, Balancing Rocks, and Snow Donuts* (The Science Behind Natural Phenomena). North Mankato, MN: Capstone Press, 2016.

Rocks, Minerals, and Gems. New York, NY: Scholastic, 2016.

Websites

Find out more about the inside of Earth at:
http://science.nationalgeographic.com/science/earth/inside -the-earth

Carry out your own fossil dig at:
http://paleobiology.si.edu/dinosaurs/interactives/dig/dinodig.html

Explore the structure of Earth at:
www.dkfindout.com/uk/earth/structure-earth

Index